Bunny with a Toolbelt's

aRfaBet

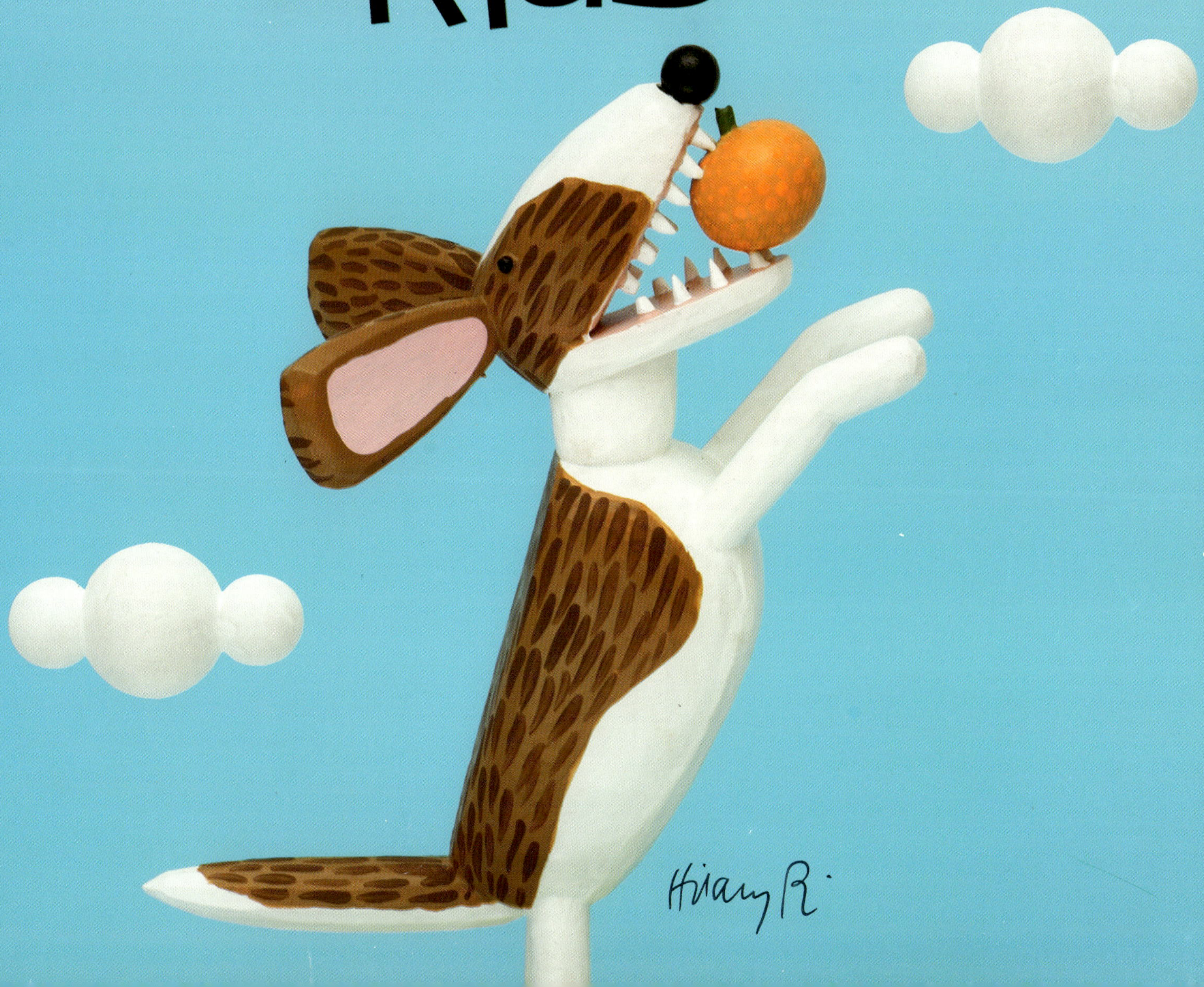

for Weegee

A

is for Astrid,
a dog with a smile.
Her angel food cake
had artistic style.

A! An Afghan Hound with an Appetite!

B

was a beagle
named Bella McGee.
She dreamed about bagels
with poppy seed fleas.

B! A Bagel-shaped Beagle!

C

is for Calder
who delivered the cheese.
His diminutive size
let him skateboard with ease.

C! A Chihuahua Cheese Courier!

D

is for Daisy
who could eat her
own weight
if a big Dagwood sandwich
appeared on her plate.

D! A Delicious Dachshund!

E

is for Edsel
whose tastes
were refined.
He liked to sip Earl Grey
tea when he dined.

E! An Epicurean English Bulldog!

F

is for Fifi
whose temper
turned jolly
when frolicking 'round
with her flying farfalle.

F! A French Poodle who Feasts on Fun!

G

is for Gilda,
whose tastes
were extreme.
She ate so many
gherkins,
her fur turned
bright green!

G! A Gastronomic Greyhound!

H

is for Homer
who's inclined
for the cold,
so he ate habaneros
by the threefold.

H! A Husky who loves Hot stuff!

I is for Izzy,
a Zen yoga master.
His penchant for
ice cream
made his routines
go faster.

I! An Irish Setter Idealist!

J

is for Jethro
who may be small fry,
but he ate a whole
Jackfruit
in 3 or 4 tries.

J! A Jack Russell Juggernaut!

K

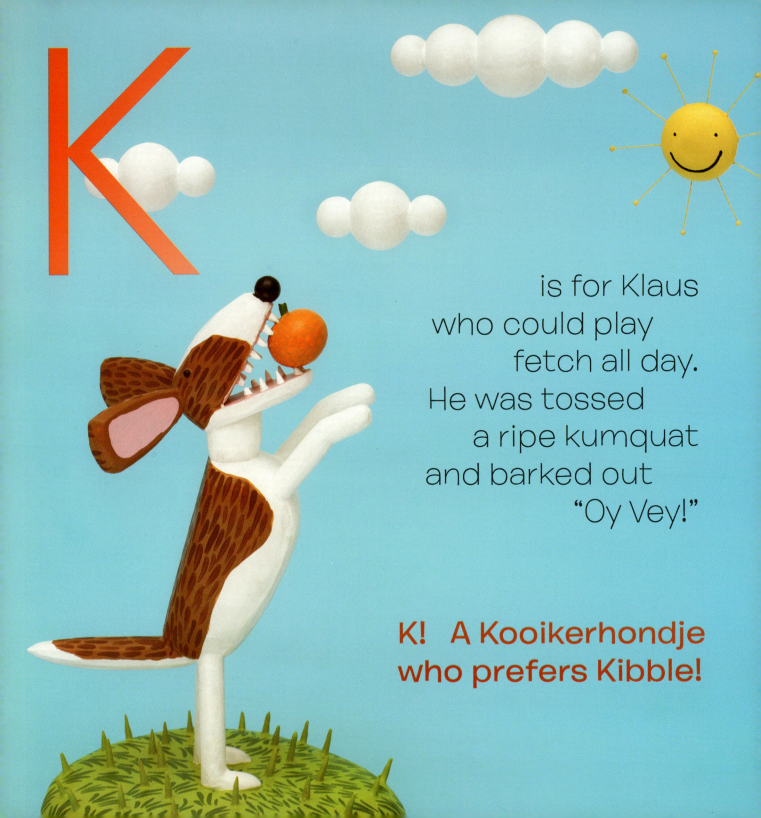

is for Klaus
who could play
fetch all day.
He was tossed
a ripe kumquat
and barked out
"Oy Vey!"

**K! A Kooikerhondje
who prefers Kibble!**

L

is for Lulu
who licked all
within reach.
She turned into
licorice--
yes, even her
leash!

L! A Labrador who Loves to Lick!

M

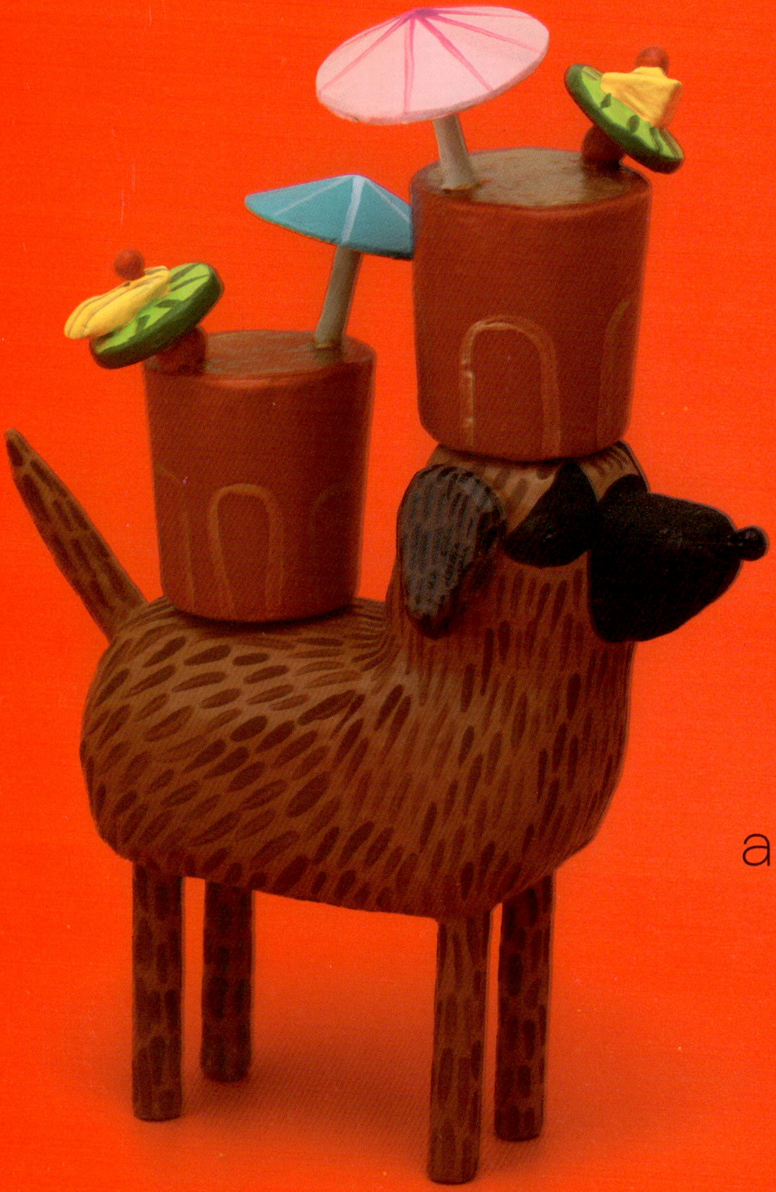

is for Marvin
who fetched
for his masters
a couple of Mai Tais
with no spillage
disasters.

M! A Mastiff with Magnificent Motor skills!

N

is for Nestor,
a champion cur.
His nonpareil fixation
was shown in his fur.

N! A Norfolk Terrier who Nibbles!

O

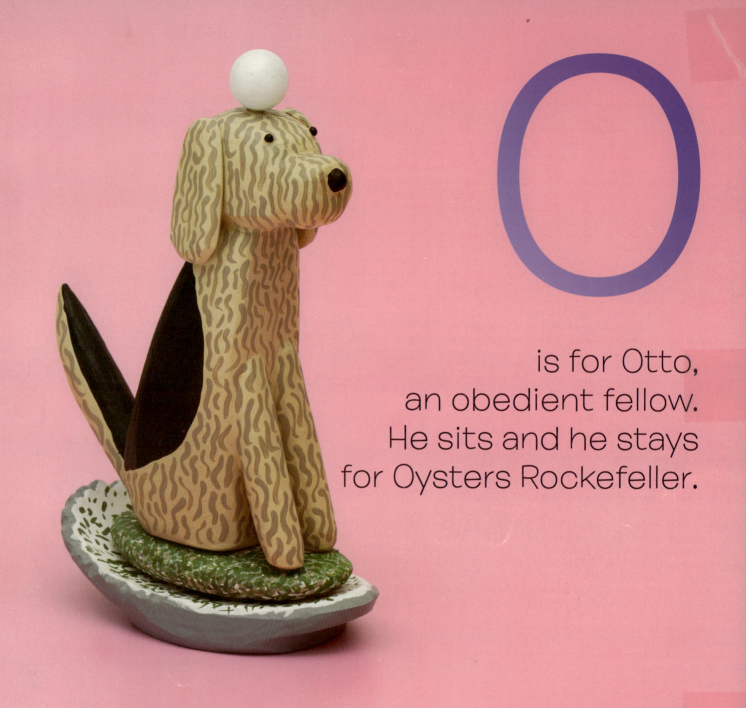

is for Otto,
an obedient fellow.
He sits and he stays
for Oysters Rockefeller.

O! Observe the Obedient Otterhound!

P

is for Pippa,
a pug from the
pound,
on a pile of
persimmons
she'd chase her
tail 'round.

P! A Pug with a Penchant for Peril!

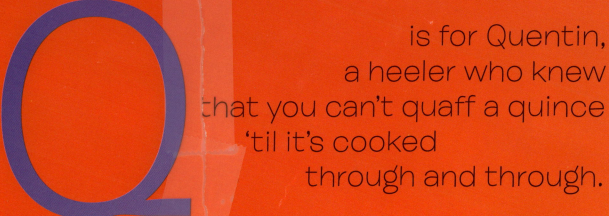

Q is for Quentin,
a heeler who knew
that you can't quaff a quince
'til it's cooked
through and through.

Q! A Queensland Heeler with Quick wits!

R

is for Raul,
whose eyes
got all dewy
when he shopped
for the makings
for his
ratatouille.

[illegible] A Russian Wolfhound with Refined tastes!

S

is for Suki,
whose great
facial hair
obscured the sashimi
on her derrière.

S! A Scottie who Savors the flavor!

T

is for Tenzing,
who was in a
kerfuffle.
While sniffing the
daisies
he discovered fresh
truffles.

T! A Taigan with well-Tempered Tastebuds!

U was Uriah
whose Udon beehive
was a perch for
bald eagles.
(And that is no jive.)

U! An Unflappable Utonagan!

V

is for Vito,
a spunky young fella
who ran through the grasses
that smelled of vanilla.

V! A Vivacious Vizsla!

W

is for Waldo,
whose waffle
fixation
meant he peed
sticky syrup,
which increased
isolation.

W! A Whippet with Wafflelust!

X

is for Xylon,
who straddled
a xouba
and rode
the big waves
while playing
the tuba.

X! a Xoloitzcuintli with eXquisite taste!

Y

is for Yma
who loved
cushy bedding,
her tiny tush fit
inside a Yorkshire
Pudding!

Y!
A Yummy
Yorkie!

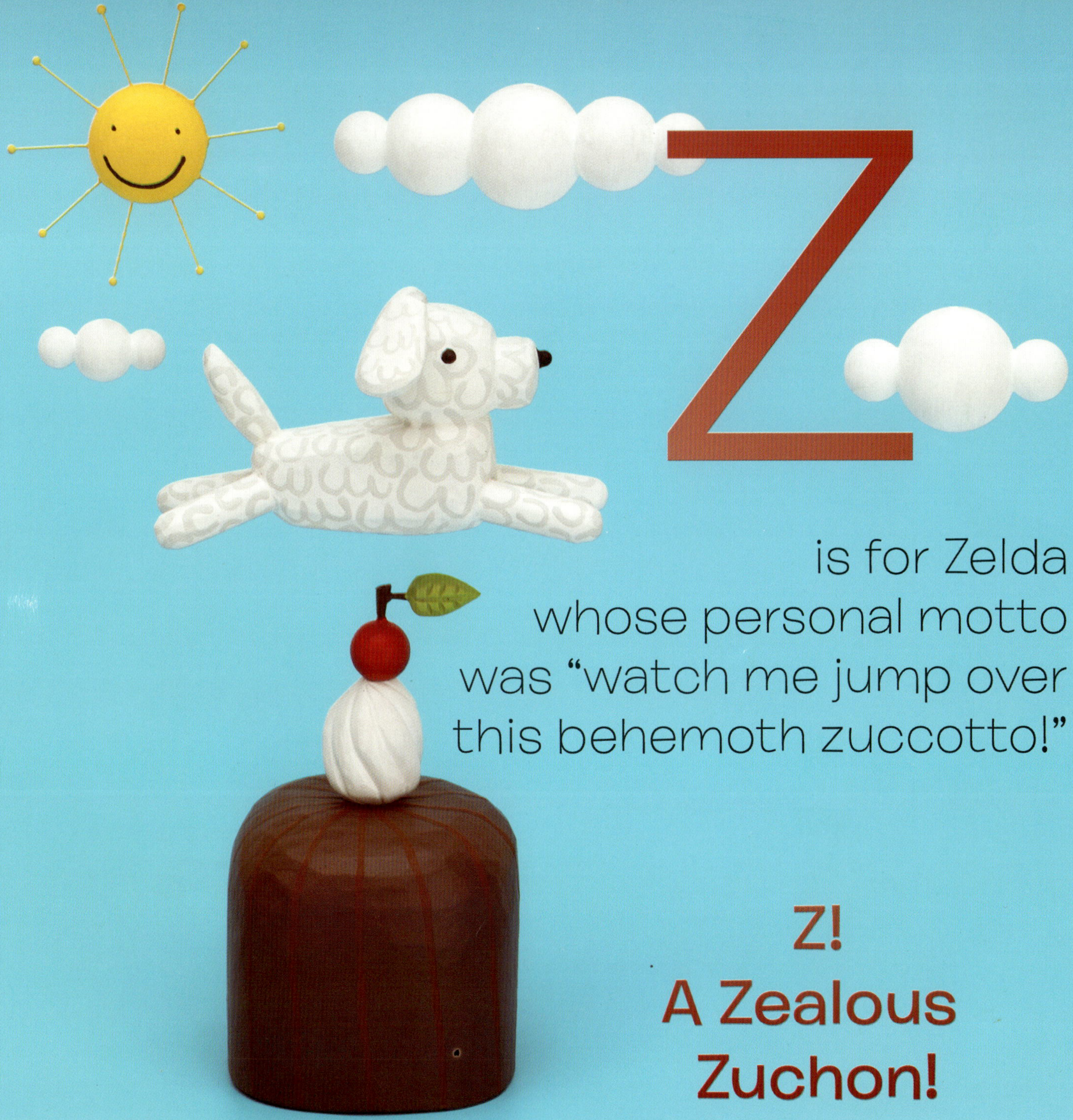

Z

is for Zelda
whose personal motto
was “watch me jump over
this behemoth zuccotto!”

**Z!
A Zealous
Zuchon!**

The Foods and Breeds of Arfabet:

Afghan Hound: One of the oldest recognizable types of dogs, this breed is known for its extremely long coat of hair.
Angel Food Cake: A kind of sponge cake named for its airy lightness.

Beagle: A medium-sized dog known for its excellent sense of smell.
Bagel: A bread ring that's first boiled, then baked.

Chihuahua: The smallest breed of dog, originally from Mexico.
There are hundreds of types of **cheese** in the world. The ones seen here include: brie, cheddar, gouda, edam, swiss, olivet au foin, a filetta, and roquefort.

Dachshund: A short-legged, long-bodied dog. In German, the name literally translates to "badger dog," although they are often nicknamed weiner dog due to the shape of their body.
Dagwood: A tall, multi-layered sandwich made with a variety of meats and cheeses. It was originally named for Dagwood from the comic strip Blondie, a character who frequently made huge sandwiches.

English Bulldog: One of many types of Bulldog, known for their stocky muscularity and very short muzzle.
Earl Grey Tea: A black tea with a distinctive flavor due to the addition of oil extracted from the rind of bergamot, a fragrant citrus fruit.

French Poodle: A breed that's actually from Germany! Poodles are known for their curly hair and high intelligence.
Farfalle: A type of pasta, named for the Italian word for butterfly.

Greyhound: A gentle breed whose long legs and narrow body allow them to reach speeds of 43 mi. or 70 km. per hour!
Gherkin: A type of pickle, originally from West Africa.

Husky: A general name for a type of dog used to pull sleds in northern regions.
Habanero Chili: One of the hottest chili peppers, originally from Mexico.

Irish Setter: A friendly dog that has a long red or brownish coat of hair.
Ice Cream: A frozen dessert treat that has its origins in ancient Persia.

Jack Russell Terrier: A small, energetic dog originally bred in England in the 19th century for hunting.
Jackfruit: Fruit from a large tropical tree, that can weigh up to 70 pounds.

Kooikerhondje: A small dog of Dutch origin. (pronounced "Koy-Ker-Hond")
Kumquat: A small oblong citrus fruit with a sweet rind and an acidic pulp.

Labrador Retriever: A dog whose paws are webbed for swimming, so they were originally bred to retrieve nets for fishermen. Their gentle temperaments make them perfect to help people who are blind.
Licorice: A plant in the legume family, the root of which is extracted and used to flavor candy or tea.

Mastiff: A type of large dog often used as a guard dog that comes in many breeds, often used as a guard dog.
Mai Tai: An alcoholic cocktail which usually contains rum, lime juice, and Curaçao liqueur. The name derives from the Tahitian word for "good."

Norfolk Terrier: A small British dog originally bred to rid barns of vermin.
Nonpareil: A small bead of colored sugar used to decorate cakes, cookies and candies.

Otterhound: A large, curly-haired dog that can hunt on land and in water.
Oysters Rockefeller: Originally created in New Orleans in 1899, this dish combines oysters on the half shell with other ingredients such as parsley, butter and bread crumbs.

Pug: A toy dog with a wrinkly, short-muzzled face and a curly tail.
Persimmon: A sweet fruit of Japanese origin.

Queensland Heeler: Also known as an Australian Cattle Dog, this dog was bred to drive cattle over long, rough distances.
Quince: A fruit used chiefly for making jelly or preserves, and never eaten raw.

Russian Wolfhound: Also called a Borzoi, this breed is generally described as a "long-haired greyhound."
Ratatouille: A vegetable casserole made of tomatoes, eggplant, peppers and other vegetables that is stewed very slowly.

Scottie: or Scottish Terrier, this breed is well-known for its distinctive shape
Sashimi: A Japanese dish of thin slices of fresh raw fish.

Taigan: A breed found in Northern Africa and Central Asia, they were a nomadic dog well-adapted to alpine regions.
Truffle: An edible fungi that grows underground or near the roots of trees and are valued as a delicacy.

Utonagan: A breed of dog that resembles a wolf, but is a mix of three breeds of domestic dog–Alaskan Malamute, German Shepherd, and Siberian Husky.
Udon noodles: A type of thick wheat-flour noodles in Japanese cuisine.

Vizsla: A short-coated hunting breed, originally from Hungary
Vanilla: A flavoring originally derived from the seed pods of Mexican orchids, Vanilla is the second most expensive spice in the world (after saffron.)

Whippet: Another racing dog, though smaller than the Greyhound. Even though they are among the fastest dogs in the world, Whippets are happy to spend most of the day at rest.
Waffle: A breakfast cake, known for its distinctive grid pattern with deep pockets perfect for holding toppings like butter or syrup. The history of the waffle can be braced to ancient Greece.

Xoloitzcuintli: A rare, hairless breed of dog also known as the Mexican Hairless Dog. (pronounced "sho-lo-itz-queen-tlee")
Xouba: A small sardine-like fish found near Spain.

Yorkie: The nickname for a Yorkshire Terrier, this dog does not shed hair as much as other dog breeds, so is a perfect pet for those with dander allergies.
Yorkshire Pudding: A light pastry made with meat drippings that originated in England.

Zuchon: A mix of Bichon Frise and Shih Tzu breeds.
Zuccotto: A chilled Italian dessert made with brandy, cake and ice cream.

Bunny with a Toolbelt is the Portland, Oregon, USA business of artist Hilary Pfeifer. Using over 90% recycled materials, Bunny with a Toolbelt creates original wedding cake toppers, nativity sets, and many other happy critters to help you celebrate just about anything. You can watch stop action animations, see images from exhibitions, enter a contest, sign up for the email list, and see much much more at
www.bunnywithatoolbelt.com

Arfabet is also available as a stop action animation, as well as a workbook where you can challenge yourself to try out the foods you learned about in this book!
Visit bunnywithatoolbelt.com for more information!

This book is dedicated to Weegee, my sweet mutt who's immortalized on the first page.

Thanks to the beautiful people who supported this project via Kickstarter.
I couldn't have done it without you!

Elephabet was conceived, designed and created by Hilary Pfeifer
Super duper photographs by Dan Kvitka. Expertly proofread by Janet Harris
The text type is Burbank by House Industries.

ISBN 978-0-9847736-1-9 LCCN: 2012913045

Printed in China
CPSIA Section 103 Compliant
www.beaconstar.com/ consumer
ID: M0120374. Tracking No.: M308621-1-8934

first edition